Dropbox In 30 Minutes

By Ian Lamont

Table Of Contents

Introduction

Got 30 minutes to spare? Good — it's all you'll need to master the basics of Dropbox!

Dropbox is an easy way to store and share photos, documents, spreadsheets, and other types of computer files. Much like the introduction of email, digital photography, and low-rise athletic socks, once you get the hang of Dropbox, you'll wonder how you ever got along without it.

Dropbox works by keeping identical copies of selected files on your computer(s) and Dropbox's cloud-based storage system, and ***automatically synchronizing*** them over an encrypted Internet connection. I've put asterisks around "automatically synchronizing," because this is the killer feature of Dropbox, something that will save lots of time and streamline collaboration. It's cited repeatedly in this guide.

What does Dropbox's automatic syncing feature enable? Here are some common scenarios:

- Mark uses Dropbox to **share a folder full of documents with four coworkers**, so they can work on spreadsheets and other documents together.

- Jennifer **backs up the photos that she takes on her iPhone, without using cables.** She can immediately access the photos on her laptop.

- Chris instantly backs up the files he's working on in Dropbox. **If his computer crashes or is stolen, he can easily recover them**.

Besides *automatic syncing*, another advantage of Dropbox is it follows the same conventions that people already use to save files, create folders, and move stuff around on their computers. This means your Dropbox data will always appear in the familiar "My Computer" (Windows) or Finder (Mac) on your computer. As a result, Dropbox is very easy to learn.

But is Dropbox right for you? Ask yourself if any of the following statements apply to your own technology practices:

- You back up files by emailing them to yourself.
- You transfer files between two computers using a USB drive.
- You want a better way to store and manage digital photos.
- You need to collaborate on documents and share files with coworkers.
- You're a total klutz who is apt to lose all of the important data on your laptop by dropping it into the swimming pool.

If you found yourself nodding as you read this list, then Dropbox will be an extremely useful utility and time-saver.

Dropbox is also a free service, although heavy users will opt to buy more storage space. But there are several official ways (as well as a few tricks) to get more free storage space, as explained in Chapter 5, "Dropbox — The Rogue FAQ". You'll find many other useful time-saving tips and ways to use Dropbox throughout the brief. The companion website (DropboxIn30Minutes.com) contains special features, including videos that demonstrate Dropbox features.

Before we get going, it's good to have a computer handy, or a smartphone, or a tablet. This way, you can quickly try out some the things discussed in this guide. Or you can just read through all of the chapters and install Dropbox later.

Let's get started with Dropbox!

CHAPTER ONE

In The Beginning: Installing Dropbox

In the introduction, I gave a brief overview of Dropbox and some of the things you can use it for. This chapter explains how to install the free version of Dropbox on computers and mobile devices. If you have already installed Dropbox, skip ahead to the next chapter (Chapter 2,   "Working With Folders/Groups Of Files"). Just make sure that if you have Dropbox installed on more than one computer or mobile device, you are logged into the same Dropbox account on all of them.

1A. Dropbox Requirements: It Works Practically Anywhere!

Unless you are using granny's 15-year old laptop running Windows 95, installing Dropbox shouldn't be a problem. It works on the following types of hardware and operating systems:

- Any PC or Mac laptop or desktop made in the last three years that has a recent version of Windows (from XP to Windows 8) or OS X (10.4/Tiger or later).

- Smartphones and tablets running the most popular mobile device operating systems — BlackBerry, Android, and Apple's iOS. This includes the iPhone and iPad, and popular Android devices made by Samsung and other manufacturers. It also includes the Kindle Fire, which runs a custom version of the Android mobile operating system.

Even if you are using an ancient laptop or PC, you should still be able to use the Dropbox website to transfer, download, and share files. That's because recent versions of the following Web browsers are all supported:

- Internet Explorer
- Firefox
- Chrome

- Safari
- Opera

Technical Requirements

Dropbox works on several Linux distributions (for hardcore geeks who can handle command-line installations; see the Dropbox website for details). Installation steps for Windows and OS X are listed below.

Dropbox's memory requirements are similar to many desktop applications. 512 MB of RAM are recommended.

More important is the amount of free storage space available on your computer's hard drive. Dropbox's website specifies "an amount of free space on your computer equal to the amount you want to store on Dropbox." If you are using the free account provided by Dropbox that comes with 2 gigabytes (GB) of storage, this means you will need 2 GB of unused storage space on each of the computers that will be linked to that Dropbox account.

Why? It's to ensure that local copies can be created on the computer that's synced to the Dropbox account. If you don't, the next time someone attempts to share a large video file of ninja cats, Dropbox may be unable to create a local copy for you to view or edit on your own computer.

In addition to desktop operating systems, Dropbox can also be installed on mobile devices, including:

- Android phones
- Android tablets
- BlackBerry devices
- iPads
- iPhones
- iPod touches
- Amazon's Kindle Fire e-readers

Smartphones don't need to have the most recent version of the mobile operating system. If the OS was installed in the last two years, you should be good. Dropbox.com publishes up-to-date system requirements for all of these platforms.

1B. Installing Dropbox

To have copies of files and folders from your Dropbox account stored on a desktop computer (PC or Mac), you will need to install the Dropbox software. For mobile devices, install the Dropbox app. Instructions are given below.

How To Install Dropbox On A PC

1. Visit Dropbox.com and click the "Download" button.

2. You will get a prompt asking what you want to do. Select "Run" when asked (see screenshot, below).

3. You will be asked whether you want to allow the installation to proceed. Click "Yes".

4. A progress bar will appear as the installation takes place.

5. Once installation is complete, you will be prompted to create a new account or enter your existing Dropbox account credentials (email address and password).

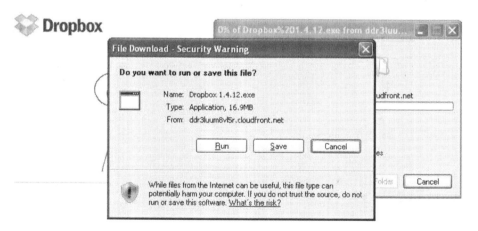

If you are a new user, you will be asked for your first and last names, your email address, password, and the name of your computer (a default is provided). Once you have filled out these fields and agreed to the Dropbox terms of service, the account will be created.

You will be presented with various installation options, including paid space, choosing the location of your primary Dropbox folder, and more. The easiest option is to go with the pre-selected options, which include the free 2 GB account and the default settings.

After installation is completed, you'll notice a Dropbox folder in Windows Explorer. It can be used like any other folder on your computer to find and transfer files (this is explained in more detail in Chapter 2: "Working With Folders/Groups Of Files").

You will also notice a Dropbox symbol on the Menu Bar (Mac) or System Tray (Windows) of your desktop (circled in the images, below), which shows whether local files in your Dropbox account have been synced to Dropbox's remote servers. This icon is very small, but it serves several important purposes. They include:

- Showing the status of *automatic syncing*. A checkmark indicates syncing is complete, while spinning arrows shows automatic syncing is taking place. Arrows "x" means automatic syncing was stopped for some reason.
- Quickly launching the Dropbox website.

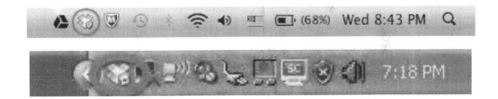

How To Install Dropbox On A Mac

Visit Dropbox.com and click the large "download" button.

The download for the installer should start automatically, but if it doesn't, click the link provided in the browser window.

You will be prompted to save the file, which will be titled something like

"Dropbox_1.6.dmg".

Go to your downloads folder or Finder and open the .dmg file you just downloaded.

A new Finder window will open up, that tells you to drag the Dropbox app into your Mac's Application folder. This should take a few seconds to complete.

Go to your applications folder and open the Dropbox app.

You will either register for or log on to Dropbox as described in the Windows installation process, above.

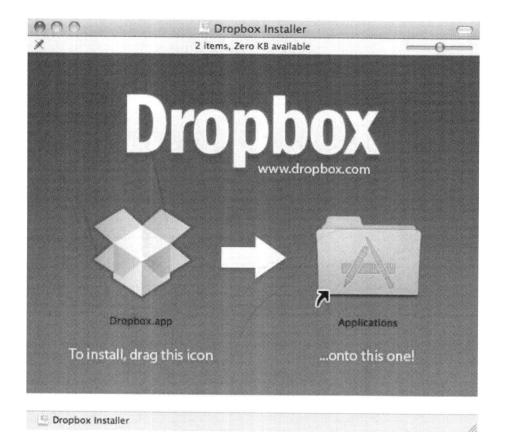

How To Install Dropbox On A Mobile Device

Apple iPhone, iPad, and iPod touch: The Dropbox app is one of the more popular apps and is easily found in the Apple App Store. Search for "Dropbox" or look in the "Productivity" category. Once selected, tap the Install button to complete the process (Note: You may need to enter your Apple iTunes password to download the app).

Android: Use the Play Store (formerly known as the Android Marketplace) to search for and download Dropbox. You'll be prompted to allow Dropbox to be installed (see screenshot below; the Android install screen is shown on the right).

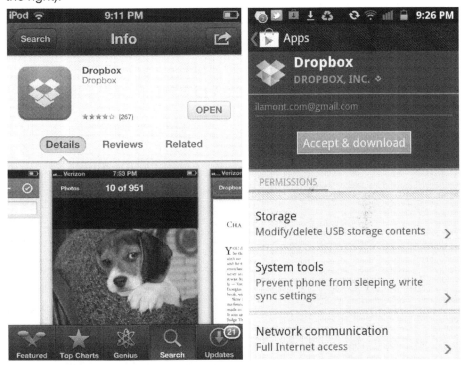

Kindle Fire: The Kindle Fire is set up to only allow apps from Amazon's app store. To disable this setting and download Dropbox, follow these instructions:

- On the Kindle Fire home screen, tap the gear icon.

- Tap More.

- Tap Device.

- Look for the Allow Installation of Applications setting. Switch it to On.

- Use the Kindle Fire's browser to visit http://www.dropbox.com/android

BlackBerry: Use your BlackBerry's Web browser to visit dropbox.com/blackberry. Select the link to download and install the Dropbox app. Reboot the device, press the Menu button and navigate to the Downloads folder to launch Dropbox.

Opening Dropbox On A Mobile Device

Once installed on your device, find the Dropbox icon and tap or select it. A new screen will appear, which will prompt you to use an existing Dropbox account or create a new one.

If you already have Dropbox installed and activated on your desktop or laptop computer, use the same account information (the email address and password you used to create the original account) in the fields provided. If this is your first time using Dropbox, create an account by filling in the fields provided.

By using the same Dropbox account on multiple computers and devices you own, it makes sharing files between them a snap.

1C. The Dropbox Website

Even if you don't have the Dropbox app installed, you can still log onto the Dropbox website at Dropbox.com to download or share files and folders.

Enquiring minds may wonder, *"Why bother with the Dropbox app if I can just use Dropbox.com to share and download stuff?"*

The answer: The website doesn't have the killer feature of *automatically syncing* your Dropbox data to your hard drive or mobile device.

I suppose you could manually download folders or files, edit them, and then manually upload them through the Dropbox website. But why torture yourself? The Dropbox app on your computer can take care of that automatically.

Here are some common uses for the Dropbox.com website:

- Accessing your Dropbox account from a friend's or colleague's computer (be sure to ask permission and pay attention to common-sense security precautions).

- Viewing a file's history, even across multiple computers and users.

- Restoring earlier versions of a file or deleted files (for example, the last version of the quarterly spreadsheet that was accidentally trashed by the dummy in accounting).

- Checking your Dropbox history (basically a reverse-chronological log of all saves, edits, and deletes).

- Changing passwords, email, and other settings, such as Facebook (why would someone want to link with Dropbox with Facebook? See the explanation in Chapter 5).

- Creating links and sharing folders (see Chapter 4, "Chapter Four - Dropbox Linking And Sharing").

CHAPTER TWO

Getting Down To Business: Files And Folders

In the introduction to this guide, I mentioned Dropbox's killer feature: *Automatically synchronizing* files. This may sound about as fun as being locked in a conference room with Bill Gates, a scientific calculator, and a bowl of stale potato chips. But trust me: It's a big deal. Besides being a major time saver, auto-synchronization unlocks some capabilities that you never imagined were possible. This chapter explains how auto-synchronization can be used to:

- Save and share files between multiple computers.
- Easy backup and recovery, even if your computer is lost, stolen, or destroyed.
- Automatically transfer photos, videos, and other files from your phone or tablet to your computer.

The first section of this chapter explains how Dropbox works conceptually, but if you simply want to learn the basics of creating files in Dropbox, sharing them among multiple computers, and accessing them from mobile devices, skip ahead a few pages.

2A. How Dropbox Works

Here is the two-minute version of How Dropbox Works on desktops and laptops. I'll skip the jargon and try to make this as painless as possible (with pictures!). So here goes.

Each free Dropbox account comes with 2 GB of free data to start. Think of this as your own master storage vault, hosted by Dropbox on remote servers connected to the Internet, but controlled by you. The remote servers are based on a technology called cloud computing. I won't get into how cloud computing works, but in the diagrams below, a cloud symbolizes Dropbox's remote servers.

Your Dropbox master storage vault is watchful, always keeping an eye on the Dropbox folder on your computer. Whenever you "drop" something into your Dropbox folder on your computer — by dragging a file into it, creating a new file, or updating an existing file — the master vault will notice and automatically synchronize, creating its own copy of that file. If the file is updated on your computer, as long as the computer is connected to the Internet, the master vault will notice and make the exact same update on *its* copy of the data. The sync process may take a few seconds or a few minutes, depending on the size of the file or update being synced. A twirling circle appears on the Dropbox icon in the System Tray (Windows) or Menu Bar (Mac) while the automatic sync is taking place. When it's done, a green checkmark will appear on the Dropbox icon.

Syncing has important implications for your data. For one, stuff that's saved to Dropbox on your computer will have a carbon copy in the master vault.

Let's use an example. Say you have a laptop made by Apple, and have installed Dropbox on it. If the laptop crashes, catches on fire, gets left on the bus, or is stolen by some light-fingered Starbucks barista while you're in the loo, that's terrible. But as long as Dropbox's automatic sync has taken place, your Dropbox files can be recovered from the master vault (more on how to do that later).

What if your laptop is not connected to the Internet, and you save something to the Dropbox folder? It will still exist locally on the computer's hard drive. The master vault won't be able to see it … yet. However, as soon the computer is reconnected to the Internet (for instance, via a known Wi-Fi network or office network) the Dropbox master vault will immediately notice what has changed in your computer's Dropbox folder. "A-ha!," it will think. "There's new stuff on the laptop that needs to be updated!" It will then automatically sync the data, so the master vault has up-to-date copies of all of the files in the Dropbox folder on the laptop.

What happens when you connect a second computer to your Dropbox account? For instance, let's say you want to use Dropbox on the Dell PC tower you use for editing video in your home office. After installing Dropbox on the Dell and logging in with your Dropbox account credentials, the PC's Dropbox folder will automatically sync to the master vault. A copy of every file and folder in the master vault will be downloaded to the Dell's hard drive. This may take a long time if a lot of data needs to be synced.

The result will be three identical copies of every file and folder associated with that Dropbox account:

1. A copy in the master vault, stored on Dropbox's servers.
2. A copy on your Apple laptop.
3. A copy on the Dell desktop.

Anytime a new file or folder is added to the Dropbox account from any device or Dropbox.com, it will be synced across all three locations. For instance, if a new file is created on the Dell PC and saved to the PC's Dropbox folder, that file will be automatically synced to the master vault as well as your Apple laptop. This relationship is shown in the inset diagram.

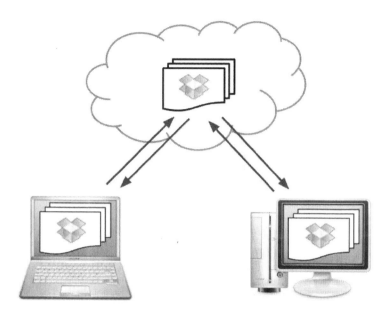

Being able to sync the same content among multiple devices provides a very convenient backup for Dropbox data. If your Mac laptop gets dropped in your backyard swimming pool, as long as it's been recently synced, you'll still be able to quickly access all of the files and folders on the desktop PC. Even if the desktop PC dies, copies of all of the files saved to Dropbox can still be downloaded from the Dropbox website. Or, you can simply buy a new computer, install Dropbox and log in to your account, and wait for *automatic syncing* to copy all of the data in your Dropbox account to the new machine.

Smartphones, tablets, and other devices associated with a Dropbox account work differently. An index of the master vault is visible on the device, but files are not downloaded unless you request them. You can manually upload files from your device to your Dropbox account, and can also set it up to automatically upload pictures and other files. This will be covered in Chapter 3, "Going Mobile".

2B. Saving Your First File

If you've followed the steps outlined in Chapter 1, you are ready to save your first file to Dropbox. It works almost exactly like saving a file on your hard drive.

How To Create A New File

1. As an example, create a new file in Word (see screenshot below) or in a text editor such as TextEdit or Notepad.

2. Type a few words of text, and save the file for the first time.

3. In the "Save" dialog window that appears, you will see the various folders in your hard drive (such as "My Documents"). A folder called Dropbox (with an imprint of the Dropbox logo on it) should be visible. Select it, name the file you are saving, and hit the "Save" button.

4. Once your computer is connected to the Internet, a spinning circle will briefly appear on the Dropbox icon in the System Tray (Windows) or Menu Bar (Mac) as your local Dropbox folder syncs to your Dropbox master vault.

5. The new file is now in Dropbox, and can be accessed by any of your other computers/devices associated with your Dropbox account.

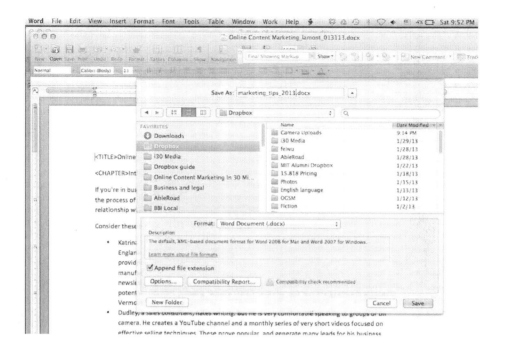

How To Place An Existing File In Dropbox

- Easiest way: Drag the file from its location on your hard drive to your Dropbox folder, using Windows Explorer or Finder.

- Alternate way: Open an existing file, and from the File menu select "Save As" or "Duplicate". Select your Dropbox folder as the new location for the saved file. To avoid confusion over which copy you are accessing (that is, the original version on your hard drive or the new version in Dropbox) you can either rename the Dropbox copy and/or delete the original.

2C. Working With Folders/Groups Of Files

Dropbox accounts can have subfolders, just like folders on your hard drive. Dropbox accounts come with a built-in folder (/Photos) but you can add your own. There are two reasons to do this:

1. Considering most people end up saving hundreds or even thousands of files to their Dropbox accounts, folders makes it easier to organize and find files in the future.

2. Folders make it possible to easily share groups of files with other Dropbox users (see Chapter 4: "Chapter Four - Dropbox Linking And Sharing").

Creating a folder in Dropbox is almost the same as creating a subfolder on your hard drive. Here are the most common methods.

Working With Existing Folders/Groups Of Files

Just as you might drag an entire folder from one location to another on your hard drive, you can do the same with Dropbox. Here's how:

1. Open two windows in Windows Explorer (Windows) or Finder (Mac).

2. Set one of them to a location on your hard drive, and the other to Dropbox.

3. Drag a subfolder containing a few small files on your hard drive to the Dropbox folder.

4. The folder will be moved from its old location on your hard drive, and added to your local Dropbox folder.

5. If your computer is connected to the Internet, you'll see the Dropbox icon in the System Tray (Windows) or Menu Bar (Mac) showing *automatic syncing* taking place, as the new folder is updated to your master vault.

6. Drag the folder back to its old location on your hard drive. Dropbox will sync again, to register the removal of the folder.

You can also copy folders or groups of files to Dropbox using Windows Explorer or Finder, as shown in the following image.

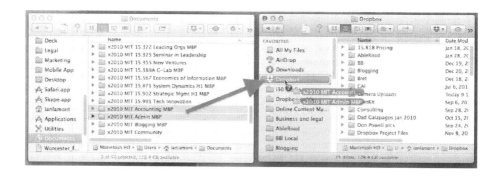

How To Create A New File In A New Folder In Dropbox

Windows

(The following instructions are based on Windows 7, but the processes will be similar for other versions of Windows.)

1. When saving a file for the first time, use the Save File dialog that comes up to navigate to the Dropbox folder.

2. In the title bar of this dialog is a link that reads "New Folder". Click it to create a new folder.

3. Save the file.

Mac/OS X

1. When saving a file for the first time, navigate to the Dropbox folder.

2. In the lower left corner of the save window is a button called "New Folder".

3. Use it to create and name a new folder within Dropbox.

How To Create A New Dropbox Folder In Windows Explorer (Windows) Or Finder (Mac)

Windows

1. You should have a Dropbox icon on your desktop from the installation process. Click on it. If you don't see it, click on the Start

button, and select "Computer" in the Windows Explorer dialog that appears.

2. Find and select Dropbox.

3. To create a new folder, click the link at the top of the dialog that says "New Folder". Or, right-click the Dropbox location, and select New, then select Folder.

Mac/OS X

1. Click the Dropbox icon in the Menu Bar.

2. From the drop-down menu that appears, choose "Open Dropbox folder" (see image, below). The Finder window for Dropbox will open.

3. In Finder, select the Perform Tasks icon (which looks like a gear).

4. A drop-down menu will appear. Pick "New Folder". Or, go to Finder > File > New Folder.

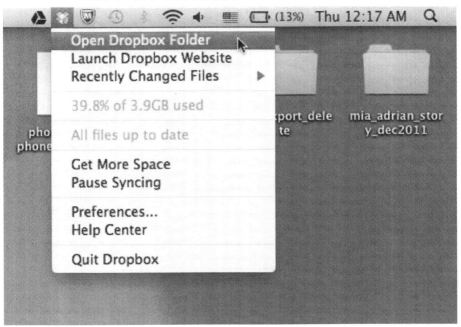

How To Create A Folder From The Dropbox Website

1. Go to Dropbox.com and log in, or click on the Dropbox icon in the System Tray (Windows) or Menu Bar (Mac) and select "Launch Dropbox Website".

2. In the top of the browser window, near the Dropbox search field, is an icon that looks like a folder with a plus symbol. Click it to create a new folder.

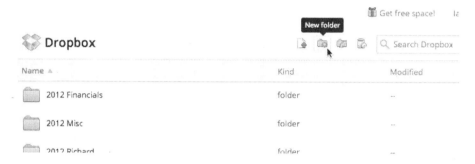

2D. Opening A File Or Folder From A Second Computer

Here's a common scenario. You're working on an important file on your desktop computer in your cubicle. Let's call it "NCAA_Office_Pool.xls". But you're traveling next week, and want to take the file with you on your laptop to continue your "work". Up until now, you may have transferred NCAA_Office_Pool.xls using the office network or USB drive, or even emailed the file to yourself to download and open up on the laptop.

Dropbox handles things differently. It's nearly effortless. As long as the Dropbox application is installed on both computers and linked to the same Dropbox account, the transfer takes place in the background, thanks to *automatic synchronization*. Setup is explained below.

How To Do It

1. Make sure the Dropbox app is installed on both computers (Note: For office computers, çheck with your IT department to determine whether Dropbox is a permitted application).

2. Log into the same Dropbox account from the Dropbox app on both computers.

3. Create the file and save it to Dropbox on the first computer.

4. Make sure the automatic sync takes place on the first computer (look for the green check mark on the Dropbox icon in the Windows System Tray/Mac Menu Bar).

5. Turn on the second computer, and check to see if the automatic sync has taken place there as well (the Dropbox icon in the System Tray or Menu Bar will have a small check on it, as shown in the image below).

6. You can now open the file on the second computer!

Any edits you make on the file will be updated on Dropbox as long as you are connected to the Internet. This means you can immediately shift back to working on the same file on the first computer, without having to manually update the file. If you add a third computer to your Dropbox account, a copy of the file will be created there as well.

There's not much else to say about transferring files between multiple computers, except to make sure the *automatic syncing* takes place on the second computer. This is a real concern if you're traveling, because you may not have easy access to a fast Internet connection to sync the latest version of the file(s) you want to edit.

For information about what happens when the same file is opened simultaneously on more than one computer, see the answer to "What happens when the same file is opened simultaneously on more than one computer?" in Chapter 5.

CHAPTER THREE

Going Mobile: Dropbox On Smartphones And Tablets

In the previous chapter, I went over the basics of handling files and folders on a computer. This chapter will discuss how to use Dropbox on a mobile device.

Smartphones and tablets extend the functionality of Dropbox. While you can't sync everything in your Dropbox account to an iPhone, 'Droid, BlackBerry, or tablet, the Dropbox mobile app makes it easy to retrieve specific files. Uploading photos and other files to Dropbox is also a breeze, thanks to the app's well-designed user interface and a feature called Camera Upload. Lastly, Dropbox has made it possible to preview photos, PDFs and other types of documents directly in the Dropbox app.

Because of differences in the Dropbox app interface among the various mobile operating systems and the frequency of mobile app updates, this chapter will concentrate on major functionality that is supported on all versions of the Dropbox app.

3A. Downloading Files

The first time you activate the Dropbox app on your device (see Chapter 1 for download and installation instructions) you will see your Dropbox folders arranged in an index. However, individual files in the folders can't be instantly accessed. That's because they are *not* automatically synced, like your Dropbox account on your desktop or laptop computer.

Hold on. No *Automatic syncing* on a smartphone or tablet? What's up with that?

The short answer: Most mobile devices don't have enough storage capacity to maintain a local copy of an entire Dropbox account. It's common to have at least a gigabyte of data in a Dropbox account, and syncing all of that data to an Android phone, iPhone, or BlackBerry would not only take up a lot of storage space, it would also take a long time to sync over a wireless connection. Instead, the mobile Dropbox app displays an index of the folders and files. Users need to manually select the files they want to download to their mobile devices, and then wait for the download to be completed over the wireless connection.

What The Icons Mean

In late 2012, Dropbox updated the look and feel of its mobile apps. New features were added, but there were also some design changes, including the removal of text labels from menu icons. Here's a quick look at the new icons on the iOS app, with explanations for what each one does:

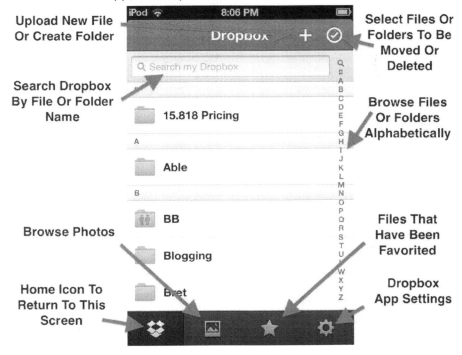

The Android Dropbox app has the same icons, with the exception of uploads, which are handled through the Android menu button (usually located below the lower left corner of the screen on Android devices).

How To Download And Open A File On Your Mobile Device

As mentioned earlier, the mobile Dropbox app does not keep a carbon copy of your entire Dropbox account. Instead, it keeps an index of all of the folders and file names. Here's how to download a particular file to your mobile device:

1. Open the Dropbox app on your device and log on (using your regular Dropbox credentials — the email address and password you used to sign up for the account).

2. Look for the Dropbox icon. Tapping this will bring up an index of the folders in your Dropbox account.

3. Navigate to the subfolder that contains the file you want to open, and select it.

4. Or, if you know the name of the file but can't remember the location, use the search function to find and select it.

5. The file may take some time to download, depending on the size of the file and the speed of the wireless connection being used.

Previewing And Sharing Files

If the file is of a type that can already be opened on your device, Dropbox will conveniently preview it for you, as shown in the screenshot below, from Dropbox's iPad app. Dropbox is previewing the image file of the boy, and by pressing the sharing icon (the rectangular icon with an arrow pointing to the right), additional sharing options are displayed:

The sharing features are very powerful, making it easy to distribute photos, PDFs, Microsoft Office files and other documents via email, Facebook, and Twitter. "Copy Link To Clipboard" creates a Dropbox URL that you can paste into email and other documents.

Some file types cannot be previewed by the mobile Dropbox app. However, once the file has been downloaded it may still be possible to open the file using another app on the device. If you see the "unable to preview" error message, tap the icon that looks like an arrow going into a rectangle (viewable in the screenshot above in the upper right corner of the screen). If there is an app that can open the file, it will be shown below the icon. Tap the app to open the file.

3B. Uploading Files

If you want to upload files to Dropbox using the Dropbox mobile app, chances are the files will be photos you've taken with the device's camera.

Dropbox has automated the upload process, using an optional feature called Camera Upload. However, the app also has a method to manually upload photos or other files. Both methods are described below.

How To Manually Upload Files Or Photos

1. From the Dropbox home screen in the app, navigate to the folder where the file is to be uploaded.

2. Tap the "+" icon and "Upload Here" button (iPad, iPhone, or iPod).

3. For Android, Kindle Fire, and other devices, tap the   menu button and "upload" option.

4. Select the files to be uploaded.

5. You may need to navigate to a location on your device or storage card to find the file you want to upload.

In the screenshot below, tapping the "+" symbol prompts the user to choose a file to upload (or a folder to create) in the "Personal" folder.

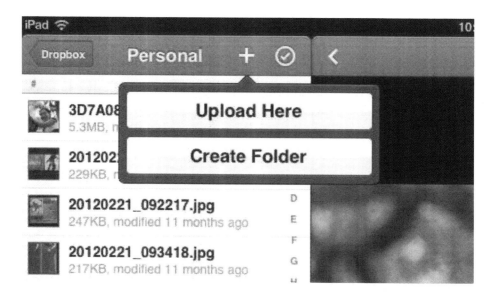

How To Automatically Upload New Photos From A Smartphone

The mobile Dropbox app has a neat feature called Camera Upload. Once activated from the app's settings, it automatically copies to Dropbox new photos and videos you create using your device's camera (and grants you some free space to boot — see Chapter 5, "How can I get free space?").

The transfer takes place when you open the Dropbox app. All accumulated photos and videos since the last time you opened the app are synced to a new folder called "Camera Upload" in your Dropbox account:

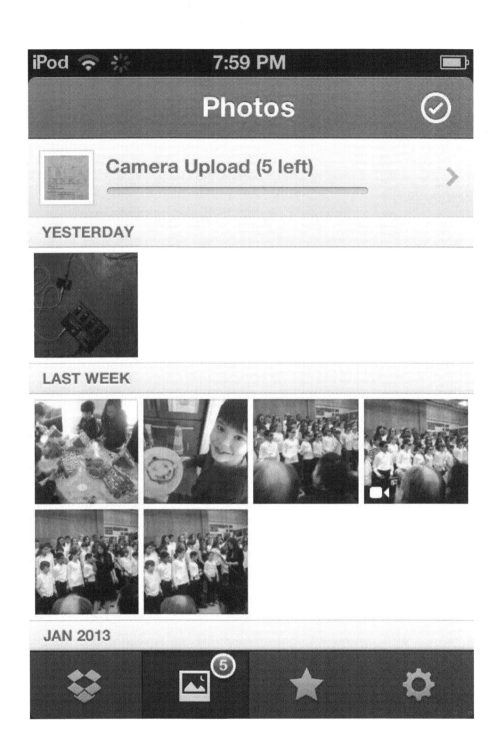

While Camera Upload is a handy feature, there are some downsides:

- If you are a smartphone shutterbug or shoot long video clips, Camera Upload can use a lot of bandwidth. Open the Dropbox app when in range of an open Wi-Fi network when possible, to avoid carrier limits and surcharges.

- You will have additional file/folder management tasks associated with the increased flow of photos and videos to your Dropbox account. For example, the files may need to be transferred out of the Camera Upload folder in order to be opened in a photo app on your PC. You may also need to regularly clear out unwanted photos on your Dropbox account.

- Video will quickly max out the free Dropbox storage space that comes with Camera Upload. While Dropbox grants some free space to users of Camera Upload, video files are so large you will either have to pay extra to get more Dropbox storage space, or start deleting old files to remain on the free plan.

CHAPTER FOUR

Dropbox Linking And Sharing

I have repeatedly mentioned the joys of Dropbox's *automatic syncing* ability. Automatic syncing may not sound very sexy, but boy, does it come with major benefits. Namely, backups are a breeze and you can easily open the same file on more than one computer, without having to manually transfer files or folders.

That's not all. Automatic syncing can also be extended to files and folders that are shared with other Dropbox users.

Here's a typical scenario: A marketing team with members in New York, San Francisco, Osaka and Paris use Dropbox to collaborate. Each has his or her own Dropbox account, but they also have access to a shared Dropbox folder that syncs with their local computers.

If one person makes a change to a document in the folder, the change will be updated across all of the Dropbox accounts that share the folder, and the computers associated with those accounts. Regardless of the time zone, country, or operating system of each team member, *automatic syncing* ensures that the shared data stays up to date.

The following chapter explains how sharing works with other Dropbox users, and how non-Dropbox users can be granted access to files in your Dropbox account.

4A. Limited Sharing Via Links

Anyone — including non-Dropbox users and random souls surfing the World Wide Web — can be granted limited access to Dropbox files and folders you select. Dropbox makes access possible by generating URLs that you can send to other people. The links look something like this:

https://www.dropbox.com/s/xydol3qki7il9v7/community_flyer.pdf

While others can view and download a file from a shared link, or make a copy of the folder/file in their own Dropbox account (if they are registered users), **changes they make to these files will not be reflected on your copy of the file in your Dropbox account**.

Note: Be very careful about the folders and files you share with others via Dropbox links. The links can be forwarded or posted online, potentially granting access to strangers who should not be able to view this data. Be sure to regularly review and remove public links, as needed (see instructions below).

How To Share Links From A Computer

1. Check to make sure your computer is connected to the Internet (required to use this feature).

2. In Windows Explorer (Windows) or Finder (Mac), navigate to your Dropbox folder.

3. Find the subfolder or file you want to share.

4. In Windows Explorer or Finder, right-click the folder or file, select Dropbox, and then select Get Link (see screenshot, below).

5. Another option in Finder: Click on the Dropbox drop-down menu in the title bar of the main Finder window, and select "Get Link".

6. The link should open up in a browser window. If it doesn't, paste the link into the browser's address bar.

7. The link can now be copied, emailed and shared with anyone. Non-Dropbox users will be able to download individual files.

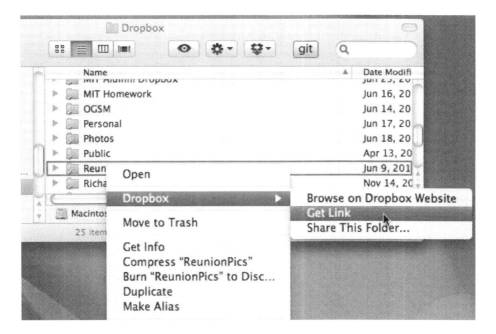

Registered Dropbox users can use a shared link to store their own Dropbox copy. However, this copy is separate from the original, and changes in the copy of the file or folder will not be updated to the original version.

How To Share Links From The Dropbox Website

- Go to Dropbox.com and log in, or launch the Dropbox website by clicking the Dropbox icon in the System Tray (Windows) or Menu Bar (Mac).

- You will be presented with a list of folders in your Dropbox account.

- To share an entire folder, hover over the name of the subfolder. A link icon will appear on the far right (see screenshot, below).

- To share a link to a single file, click the folder name and hover over the name of the file you want to share. A link icon will appear on the far right.

- Click the link icon. It will open in a new browser window.

- Copy the link from the browser address bar.
- It can now be emailed and shared with anyone.

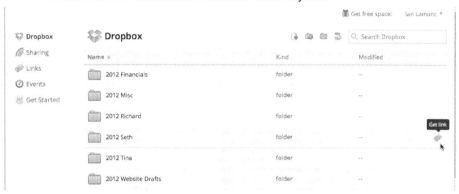

How To Share Dropbox Links From A Mobile Device

Recognizing that many people now use their mobile phones and tablets as devices for daily sharing, Dropbox has updated its Android and iOS (iPhone/iPad) apps with all kinds of sharing options. Not only can you create Dropbox links to files from your 'Droid or iPhone, it's also possible to directly share via Facebook, Twitter, texting, and email. You can also copy the link, and then manually paste it into other programs.

As you'll see from the screenshots below, the interfaces for iOS and Android look quite different. But the concept is basically the same: Locate a photo, document or other file you want to share using the Dropbox index, and then press an icon to enable sharing.

iPhone And iPad Link Sharing

On iOS devices, sharing is managed through the "forwarding" icon that you may recognize from the iPhone's or iPad's email programs. Here's how to share a link:

1. Open the Dropbox app for the iPhone or iPad, and navigate to the file you want to generate a link to.

2. 'Tap the file to open or preview it.

3. Tap the "forward" icon. On the iPad, it will be in the top right of the screen. On the iPhone or iPod touch, it will be on the lower left corner of the screen.

4. A list of sharing options will appear (see screenshots, below).

The image on the left shows the iPad view, while the image on the right shows the view for smaller iOS devices:

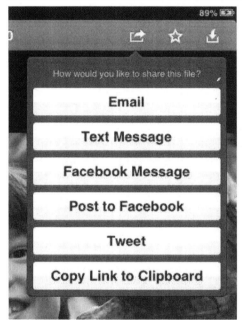 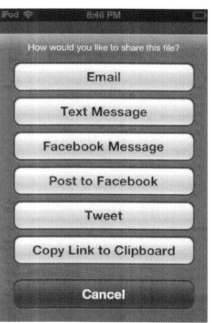

Android Link Sharing

Android offers a different interface for sharing links. Here's how to do it:

1. Open the Dropbox app for Android, and find the file or folder you want to share.

2. Tap the row containing the name of the file or folder.

3. A circle with a small triangle appears on the right side of the screen

(see screenshot, below left). Tap it.

4.   Several options appear, including an icon that is labelled "Share" (see screenshot). Tap it.

5.   Choose one of the distribution options (see screenshot, below right).

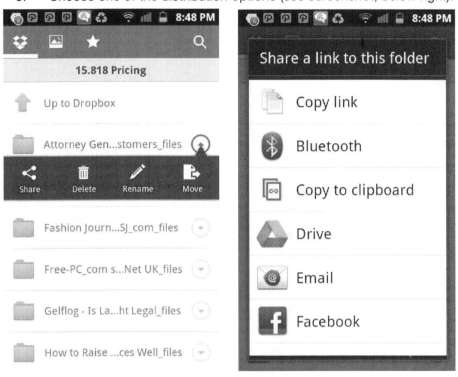

There are several extras in the Android Dropbox app that other versions do not not have, including the ability to share folders and extra distribution options.

How To Kill Links That You've Already Created Or Shared

1. Go to Dropbox.com and log in.

2. In the navigation on the left side of the browser window, select the

menu item for Links.

3. You will see a list of all of the links you have created, and an option to individually remove links you no longer want active (see image, below).

4. Note that removing the link does not delete the file.

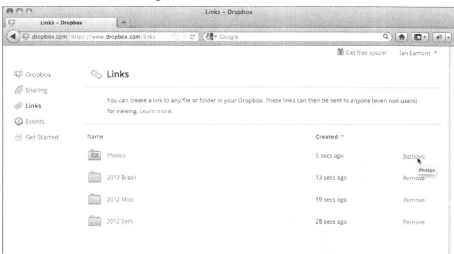

If a link is removed, it will no longer be possible to use it to access the file or folder it was associated with. However, if another Dropbox user has used a shared link to make a *copy* of a file or folder, removing the link will not remove the copy of the file or folder in that user's Dropbox account.

4B. Collaboration With Shared Folders

Sharing a folder in order to collaborate with other Dropbox users is kind of like sharing the crisper bin in a refrigerator with a broken light bulb. They'll get access to the lettuce and apples, and can even add their own produce. But they can't see what's in the rest of the fridge, and they don't have permission to drink your beer or eat your ice cream.

The refrigerator metaphor may be a bit of a stretch. Regardless, Dropbox sharing is a great way to collaborate. Unlike sharing links, which only lets other people see a file or download copies of files, Dropbox collaboration involves letting other users update documents and add new files to shared folders. However, collaborators can only access shared folders — they don't get access to anything else in your Dropbox account.

This chapter will explain how basic sharing works, and will briefly discuss some of the challenges associated with Dropbox collaboration, including managing users and storage requirements.

Collaboration via shared folders can be set up from Dropbox on your computer, but many sharing features are managed from the Dropbox website.

How To Share Folders From The Desktop

1. You'll need an Internet connection.

2. Navigate to the Dropbox folder you want to share with collaborators using Windows Explorer or Finder and select that folder (Note: You cannot share an entire Dropbox account).

3. Using the Dropbox drop-down menu (Mac) or right-clicking and selecting "Dropbox" (Windows or Mac), choose the option that says "Share This Folder …"

4. You'll be brought to the Dropbox website, which shows the folder you want to share.

5. A prompt will ask you to invite collaborators by email address or Facebook (see image, below).

6. After sending the invitations, the status of the Dropbox folder will switch to "shared". On the Dropbox website and in Windows Explorer/Finder, shared Dropbox folders have an icon that looks like two stick figures holding hands.

7. The Dropbox user receiving the invitation will get a link that leads to his or her Dropbox account online, from where they can accept or decline the invitation.

Collaboration From The Dropbox Website

1. On Dropbox.com, look for a rainbow icon. Yes, a rainbow. Don't ask why. Just know that clicking rainbows on the Dropbox website will bring you to the sharing screen.

2. Dropbox folders that have already been enabled for sharing are listed on this screen. Click the "options" link next a folder to invite additional Dropbox users to have shared access to that folder.

3. Or, click the button at the top of the screen that says "New Shared Folder" (see image, below).

4. You can select an existing subfolder, or create a new Dropbox folder to share.

5. The invitation process is completed in the same way as sharing a subfolder from a computer (see above).

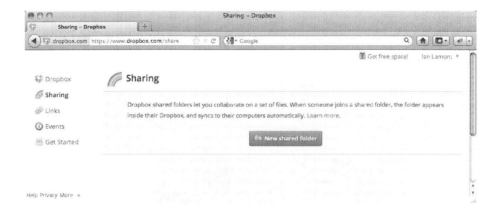

How Sharing Works

Sharing the contents of a subfolder means at least one other collaborator will be able to add, delete, or change files in that folder. It doesn't matter if the other users have different operating systems. There is no limit to the number of other Dropbox users who can share a folder. However, the more users in a folder, the bigger the risk of hitting storage limits (see "Managing shared storage space," below) or stepping on each other's toes if two people open and edit the same file simultaneously (see the answer to the question in The Rogue FAQ titled, "What happens when the same file is opened simultaneously on more than one computer?").

What To Expect

- Automatic sync means that whenever someone in a shared folder makes a change, everyone with access will see that change the next time their Dropbox accounts are synced.

- When new files are added, updated, or moved, Dropbox will show a status message informing you of the changes on your computer.

- On the Dropbox website, open a shared folder to see who has most recently accessed or changed specific files.

- Select the file and choose "More" from the options above to see the version history.

Conflicted Copies

If two people access the same file at the same time, this will cause a conflict. Both people will be able to edit it simultaneously, but using different copies of the same file.

- The first person to save his or her changes will have those changes reflected in the original file stored in the shared folder.

- The copy being used by the second person will become a "conflicted copy" with a modified name (see image, below), and placed in the same shared folder.

- Conflicted copies will have to be manually merged back into the original. This scenario is described in The Rogue FAQ.

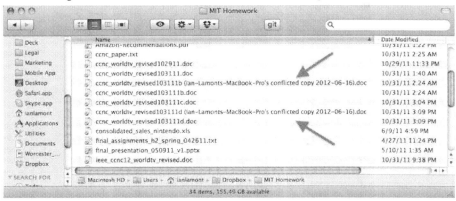

Managing Shared Storage Space

As you create shared folders in Dropbox and get invited to other people's shared folders, you'll have to contend with reduced amounts of available storage on your Dropbox account. This is because accessing a shared folder means the data in that folder comes out of your account limit. Moreover, shared folders typically grow in size as multiple members add files or make changes.

Here are some practical tips to managing your shared storage space.

How To Check Shared Folder Storage Space

1. Go to Dropbox.com. In the upper-right corner, you will see your name or Dropbox username and a drop-down menu icon. Click it.

2. Select Settings and then Account Info.

3. A graphic (see example, below) will show your total Dropbox account storage limit, and the amount that is taken by shared data and regular (unshared) data.

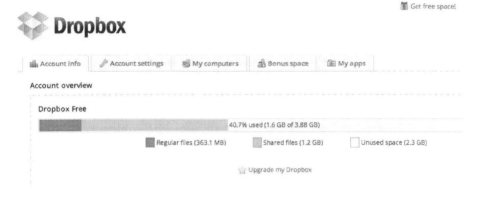

Tips For Managing Shared Storage

Over time, you may find it necessary to reduce the amount of shared folders, files, and other data.

Why? It could be your Dropbox account is approaching its storage cap, or there is no space left to add another shared folder. Here are some tips on how to approach shared storage management:

- Evaluate which folders and files are taking up the most storage space using Windows Explorer (right-click on a file or folder to select "Properties") or Mac's Finder application (right-click and use the "Get Info" command).

- Consider the age of files or subfolders. Older content is less likely to be used, shared or accessed again.

- Look for large files that may no longer be needed in Dropbox. Yes, I'm talking about the video from the shared Halloween party folder from a few years back featuring you dressed up as a circa-1978 disco dancer. I love bell-bottoms and cheap sunglasses as much as the next guy, but video files tend to be large and can really eat into your Dropbox allotment. Archive it somewhere else.

- Before deleting shared Dropbox content, check with your colleagues or other people using it — they may still need to access it. Yes, even the disco video!

- Consider unsharing or leaving a shared folder, which will free up space and give other users the options of making a copy of the shared data if they are reluctant to delete it (see below).

How To Unshare Or Leave Shared Folders

If you are the owner of a shared folder (that is, the person who created the folder and invited others to share it), you can "unshare" it. This means others will no longer be able to access it. It's also easy to leave a shared folder. Here's how:

1. Go to Dropbox.com and log in to your account.

2. Click the rainbow icon to access sharing options.

3. You will be presented with the shared Dropbox subfolders you belong to (see screenshot, below).

4. Click the Options link next to a shared folder.

5. You will see a button to leave the folder. You will also have an option to make a copy of the content in the folder.

6. Owners will also see a button to unshare the folder. Pressing this will bring up the list of other Dropbox users who are sharing the folder.

7. Next to each name is a drop-down menu with options to contact, kick out, or make that person the new owner of the shared folder.

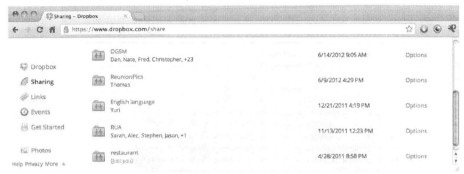

If you kick someone out of a shared folder, you will be given an option to let that person make a copy of the folder's contents. But the copy will no longer be synced to the shared folder.

CHAPTER FIVE

Dropbox: The Rogue FAQ

FAQs are frequently asked questions, typically found on company websites. I don't work for Dropbox, so I can't write an official FAQ for Dropbox.com. Nevertheless, I wanted to write an unofficial FAQ to answer important "how-to" questions. The FAQ also touches a few uncomfortable issues that Dropbox's official FAQs would never address. That's why it's called the Rogue FAQ. If you have any questions that you think should be added, contact me using the email address on the last page of this book.

How Can I Get Free Space?

People love getting free stuff. In Dropbox's case, the free stuff is virtual — storage space that can boost the size of your account. The basic free Dropbox account starts with 2 GB total, but through various methods you can double, triple, or even nonuple (I checked, that's a real word!) the total. There are also a couple of tricks to get even more space, as described below.

Here are the most popular ways to get free space:

- **Invite a friend to start using Dropbox using the Dropbox website.** If he or she signs up, you'll be awarded extra space to your free account — currently 500 MB per user, to a maximum of 18 GB (Note: if you have a Pro account, each referral comes with 1GB of additional free space). To send out invitations, go to Dropbox.com and click on the gift icon or link that says "Get Free Space." You can either do a bulk mailing from your email address book, manually type in email addresses, or use Twitter and Facebook to generate unique signup links. If people respond to any of these methods to sign up, you'll get the free space.

- **Adding Camera Upload to your account.** This feature, which automatically syncs photos on your smartphone or tablet to your

Dropbox account, comes with 500 MB of extra storage space. I've noticed it also periodically grants extra storage space if you frequently use it.

- **Jumping through various Dropbox hoops**. For instance, Dropbox gives smaller amounts of free storage to users who do things like taking the Dropbox online tour or linking to your Facebook account (see these and other examples in the image below).

Upgrade your account	50 GB	
Upgrade to Dropbox Pro to get the most space	or more	
Refer a friend to Dropbox	16 GB	
Spread the love to your friends, family, and coworkers	500 MB per friend	
Get started with Dropbox	+ 250 MB	
Take a tour of the basics of Dropbox		
Connect your Facebook account	+ 125 MB	
Share folders with your friends and family in a snap		
Connect your Twitter account	+ 125 MB	
Invite your friends to Dropbox with a tweet		
Follow Dropbox on Twitter	+ 125 MB	
Stay up to date with the latest Dropbox tweets		
Tell us why you love Dropbox	+ 125 MB	
We'd love to hear your feedback		

A few additional free space tricks

- **Set up additional Dropbox accounts**. If you have more than one email account, you can create additional Dropbox accounts. Each new account comes with 2 GB of free space. In addition, using Dropbox's invite feature on the first account to invite yourself on the second account generates extra free space for the first account. However, there are drawbacks to having multiple Dropbox accounts. The main problem: It adds additional management headaches, as the Dropbox app installed on your computer or mobile device can only be logged into one account at a time.

- Of course, there is an even easier trick to get free storage space — **delete old or unused files in your account**. Video files or old backups of entire folders are some of the biggest storage hogs, so getting rid of those can free up hundreds of megabytes at a time. Of course, if it's a shared folder, always ask your other collaborators before deleting data. Or, simply leave the folder.

How Secure Is Dropbox?

This can be an uncomfortable question for Dropbox users who save sensitive files or other valuable data in their accounts. Think of business plans, legal documents, financial projections and, er, personal photos that you wouldn't want to fall into unfriendly hands. This data is stored in "the cloud" — remote Internet servers that neither you nor Dropbox fully controls.

While Dropbox goes through great lengths to reassure users that it takes security seriously (it says it uses technologies like Secure Sockets Layer and heavy-duty encryption, and claims employees are prohibited from viewing the content of users' files) there have been security incidents, including a bug that allowed any Dropbox account to briefly be accessible without passwords in June 2011. The company quickly fixed the problem and claims additional safeguards were put in place. The company now offers the option of using two-factor identification. Nevertheless, there is no guarantee that some other bug, error, or hack might expose Dropbox user data in the future.

In addition, Dropbox users themselves may be the source of problems. If you are sharing a folder with 100 users, a couple of them are bound to be using easily guessed passwords to guard their accounts (the names of pets or first-born children, "password", etc.). Sharing links can also lead to problems, if the wrong link is shared or someone posts the link online or in some other public forum.

Despite these issues, millions of people use Dropbox every day. They're aware that there's a risk, but are basically making a tradeoff. They are putting more value on the convenience of accessing and sharing files over the Internet for free (or for a low cost), and discounting the chances that the data may be lost, stolen, or exposed.

As I said earlier, it's an uncomfortable feeling for some people. If it's too much for you, don't use Dropbox — or only use it for non-sensitive data.

What Happens When I Quit Dropbox From The System Tray (Windows) Or Menu Bar (Mac)?

When you "quit" Dropbox, you will still be able to access the Dropbox folders on your hard drive. This means you can open files, and save new files to the Dropbox folders. However, syncing will no longer take place — if you create a new file and save it to a Dropbox folder on your computer's hard drive, it won't be synced to your master account on Dropbox's servers. Conversely, the Dropbox folder on your computer won't register changes made to the master account, including new files or updates made via the Dropbox app on your mobile device or shared folders.

To restart Dropbox, find the application on your computer and double-click it. You may need to log back in, using your existing Dropbox credentials (email address and password).

How Do I Delete Dropbox?

Deleting Dropbox can be as hard as killing a vampire. You may think normal methods are enough to do the job. But just when you think you're done, it pops up alive and kicking in some other place.

You can easily delete the Dropbox application from your computer, just as you would any other application. But the Dropbox folders still remain on your hard drive. To get rid of those folders and the files in them, drag and drop them to your trash on your desktop. Note that this will not completely erase the data from your hard drive. To do that, you will need to use a special utility — Google "permanently delete files" to learn more.

In addition, once you have deleted the Dropbox application and folders from your computer, the data will *still* live on wherever you have the Dropbox application installed — other computers, your smartphone, your tablet — as well as in your Dropbox master vault, stored on Dropbox's cloud servers.

It's time to break out the wooden stakes, garlic, and other tools to kill the Dropbox vampire for good. Go after the other computers and mobile devices first. Uninstall the app, then trash and wipe the data. Then you'll need to delete your Dropbox account, using the instructions and special link in Dropbox.com's help section.

Note that you can permanently delete selected files via the Dropbox website, and the changes will be reflected on the PCs and devices that have the Dropbox app installed. Visit Dropbox.com and search for "delete Dropbox", and you will be able to click on a link to guide you through the process.

Help! I Accidentally Deleted An Important File!

If your account is active, and you deleted the file within the last few weeks, you can retrieve the file. Go to the Dropbox website, and click the trashcan icon near the top of the screen. Deleted folders and files will now be shown as grayed-out names as you navigate around the website. Right-click on a deleted file or folder to restore it, or permanently delete it.

Earlier versions of files can also be recovered. To see the history of a particular file and open an earlier version, follow these steps:

1.   Log on to the Dropbox website.

2.   Find the file in question.

3.   Right-click on the file and select the Previous Versions option.

4.   You will see the previous versions of the file created in the last 30 days.

5.   Select the version you wish to see, and click the Restore button.

Here's the view of the Previous Versions of a text file:

Version history of 'scrivener_production_notes_092012.txt'

Dropbox keeps a snapshot every time you save a file. You can preview and restore 'scrivener_production_notes_092012.txt' by choosing one of the versions below:

	Version 5 (current)		Edited by Ian Lamont (Ian-Lamonts-MacBook-Pro)	2/2/2013 12:02 PM	5.96 KB
◉	Version 4		Edited by Ian Lamont (Ian-Lamonts-MacBook-Pro)	2/2/2013 12:02 PM	5.89 KB
○	Version 3		Edited by Ian Lamont (Ian-Lamonts-MacBook-Pro)	2/2/2013 12:00 PM	5.73 KB
○	Version 2		Edited by Ian Lamont (Ian-Lamonts-MacBook-Pro)	2/2/2013 12:00 PM	5.64 KB
○	Version 1		Edited by Ian Lamont (Ian-Lamonts-MacBook-Pro)	2/2/2013 12:00 PM	5.63 KB
○	Version 0 (oldest)		Added by Ian Lamont (Ian's iMac)	1/3/2013 8:51 AM	5.6 KB

Note that Dropbox keeps deleted files as well as earlier versions of files for 30 days. If you want to set up your account to keep all versions of old files, Dropbox has a paid feature called Packrat (explained in the next FAQ question).

What does Dropbox's Packrat feature do?

Here's the scenario. You have been working on a report for the past three months, and are dealing with a particularly tough section on widget design. All of a sudden, you realize that you actually wrote an extra chapter that covers this very issue. That was two months ago. You deleted the chapter because you thought you wouldn't need it. Now you do. Is it possible to retrieve the chapter?

The answer: It depends. If you are using Packrat, a paid Dropbox feature, you can retrieve an earlier version of a file, or a deleted version of a file, no matter how old it is.

But if you are using the free version of Dropbox, you're out of luck. Dropbox keeps a 30-day history of old versions of files (as well as deleted files), but anything older than 30 days will be wiped permanently from Dropbox's servers.

In addition, Packrat is not retroactive. Meaning, even if you upgrade to Packrat, you won't be able to access older versions of files that passed the 30-day mark under the free plan.

How much does Packrat cost? If you upgrade to any Dropbox Pro plan (starting at $100 per year), you can pay an additional $39 per year to have Packrat. If your company uses Dropbox For Teams, Packrat is free.

Dropbox Seems To Be Taking A Long Time To Sync. What Gives?

If you are installing Dropbox for the first time on a new computer, and you log into an existing account with more than 1 GB of stored data, it will take a long time to sync — more than 15 minutes is typical, even on a fast network. For instance, I recently installed Dropbox on a desktop computer and synced my Dropbox account with 1.6 GB of data over an extremely fast fiber network. It took just over 30 minutes to complete.

If you are syncing just a few small files across a weak network connection, Dropbox may also seem slow. In such cases, it may be best to wait until you are near a faster Wi-Fi or wired Internet connection. To pause Dropbox temporarily (useful on a slow connection), go to the Dropbox icon in the System Tray (Windows) or Menu Bar (Mac) and select "Pause Syncing".

I See A Folder Called "Public" In My Dropbox Account. What's That?

Before 2012, the content of Dropbox folders could not be linked unless it was in a specially designated "Public" folder. The Public folder was created automatically when a user first registered with the service.

The Public folder became unnecessary when Dropbox added the ability to share links to any folder or file. Old Dropbox accounts still have public folders, new accounts don't.

What Happens When The Same File Is Opened Simultaneously On More Than One Computer?

There are two scenarios where this typically occurs:

1. You are working on two computers and open the same file on one computer before saving it on the other computer.

2. You are accessing a file in a shared folder, and someone else opens it at the same time.

In either case, there are two copies of the same file simultaneously being worked on. Differences are being introduced to each copy. How does Dropbox resolve this?

The short answer: Dropbox doesn't resolve this. It can't.

However, Dropbox at least lets you know there's a problem. The first copy to be saved keeps the original name, while Dropbox will save the second copy with "conflicted" and a bunch of numbers added to the file name. It will be up to you or another Dropbox user (if it's a shared folder) to manually merge the two files.

Trust me, manual merges are not fun. The way I have handled this in the past is by performing side-by-side reviews, copying and pasting, and pulling out large tufts of hair. Sometimes I have had to drag other people back into the mess, asking team members using the shared folder to give the file in question another review.

Clearly, this is a problem in need of a solution. I hope Dropbox (or independent developers working with the Dropbox API/SDK, see below) can figure out a technical fix. In the meantime, coordination of edits via email, IM, Yammer, or other tools can help prevent this situation from arising.

Are The Paid Dropbox Accounts Worth It?

For people who do a lot of online collaboration requiring shared files or folders, Dropbox Pro accounts are definitely worth it. For $10/month or $100/year, you can get 100 GB of storage. There is also a Team account, which comes with even more storage as well as extra administrative options. It starts at $800 for five users.

For individual users who don't do much sharing with other people, Pro accounts are less of a value. For the cost of a yearly Dropbox Pro account, one could buy several terabytes of hard disk storage. On the other hand, the convenience of *automatic syncing* between multiple computers and painlessly transferring photos from phones may be worth it for those users who have more than a few gigabytes of data to deal with.

Why Would I Want To Link My Facebook Account To Dropbox?

I can understand sharing photos, links to news articles, and even PetVille updates on Facebook. But adding Dropbox updates to your timeline? Why would anybody select this option?

Facebook sharing doesn't seem to be as much of a benefit to users as it is to Dropbox, which wants to get more people to sign up to use the service. The idea is, if it's easier for people to share links and folders with their Facebook contacts, Dropbox will get more users clicking on Dropbox content, and some of them will eventually convert to paid Dropbox accounts.

This may appeal to some people. But others may not want the contents of their Dropbox folders showing up on their Facebook feeds. I certainly don't.

There are also security considerations — what if someone you know has their Facebook account hacked, and all of a sudden those Dropbox links are visible to strangers?

My advice: Don't activate Facebook sharing unless you have a pressing need to do so. There are many other ways of sharing links and folders, as described in Chapter 4.

What Are Third-Party Apps, And How Do They Relate To Dropbox?

Third-party apps are software programs that leverage Dropbox in some way, but aren't made by Dropbox.

Independent software developers and other companies have the ability to create new services that can access or leverage Dropbox features. They do this via Dropbox's software development kit (SDK) and Application Programming Interface (API). The third-party apps generally address limitations of the Dropbox service or enhance the functionality of another app.

For instance, Otixo serves as a single interface and transfer point for Dropbox and other online storage services, such as Google Docs, Box, SkyDrive and even FTP servers. Another example: If you are a WordPress blogger, there are many Dropbox-based plugins that create upload forms, backup processes, and even content delivery networks to handle hosting of files.

The list of third-party Dropbox apps, extensions and plug-ins is large and growing every week. Use Google to find them. Or, check the support pages of services you already use to see if there is a way to leverage your Dropbox account.

Credits

All photos and screenshots were taken by the author in 2012 and 2013. The computer icons that appear in the diagrams in Chapter 2 were sourced from the Open Icon Library and are used under the terms of a Creative Commons License (CC-BY-SA 3.0).

The cover design is by Steve Sauer of Single Fin design.

Thanks to Sindya Bhanoo, Bret Siarkowski, and Chris Tompkins for reading early drafts and giving suggestions about how to improve this guide. Jeff Orkin kindly donated a laptop for testing Dropbox in Windows.

About The Author

Ian Lamont is an author and digital media entrepreneur. His media career has spanned more than 20 years across three continents, including a stint in the British music business and a six-year residence in Taipei, where he learned Mandarin and worked for a local TV network and newspaper.

It was while living overseas that Lamont encountered the World Wide Web for the first time. He was immediately inspired by the power of this new platform, and set about learning HTML and other online technologies. His career soon transitioned to the digital realm. He built websites for Harvard University, and designed new online services and managed online editorial teams for several tech news publications. He was the senior editor, new media for IDG's *Computerworld* and served as the managing editor of *The Industry Standard*. Later, he founded two start-up ventures, including a mobile software company and i30 Media Corporation.

Lamont has written for more than a dozen publications, including *Computerworld*, *The Economist Intelligence Unit* and the BBC World Service. His writing and editorial work has garnered awards from the Society of American Business Editors and Writers, the American Society of Business Publication Editors, and the Trade Association and Business Publications International. He has authored several books, including *Dropbox In 30 Minutes*, *Google Drive & Docs In 30 Minutes*, and *Excel Basics In 30 Minutes*.

Lamont is a graduate of the Boston University College of Communication, the Harvard Extension School, and MIT's Sloan Fellows Program in Innovation and Global Leadership.

Connect Online

Official Book Website: DropboxIn30Minutes.com

In 30 Minutes™ on Twitter: @in30minutes

Ian Lamont on Twitter: @ilamont

Email: ian@in30minutes.com

Bonus: Introduction to Google Docs And Drive In 30 Minutes

*(If you liked **Dropbox In 30 Minutes**, you may also be interested in **Google Drive & Docs In 30 Minutes**. The following bonus chapter is the introduction to the book. If you're interested in learning more about the book, visit DriveDocsIn30Minutes.com.)*

Thanks for your interest in *Google Drive & Docs In 30 Minutes*. I wrote this unofficial user guide to help people get up to speed with Google Docs, a remarkable (and free) online office suite that includes a word processor (Documents), spreadsheet program (Spreadsheets), and slideshow tool (Presentations). The guide also covers Google Drive, which can be used for online and offline file storage. Google Drive and Docs are presented as an integrated software suite.

How do people use Google Drive and Docs? There are many possible uses. Consider these examples:

- **A harried product manager needs to continue work on an important proposal over the weekend.** In the past, she would have dug around in her purse to look for an old USB drive she uses for transferring files. Or, she might have emailed herself an attachment to open at home. Instead, she saves the Word document and an Excel spreadsheet to Google Drive at the office. Later that evening, on her home PC, she opens her Google Drive folder to access the Excel file. All of her saves are updated to Google Drive. When she returns to work the following Monday, the updated data can be viewed on her workstation.

- **The organizer of a family reunion wants to survey 34 cousins** about attendance, lodging preferences, and potluck dinner preparation (always a challenge — the Nebraska branch of the family won't eat corn or Garbanzo beans). He emails everyone a link to a Google Docs Web Form. The answers are automatically transferred to Google Spreadsheets, where he can see the

61

responses and tally the results.

- A small business consultant is helping the owner of Slappy's Canadian Diner (*"We Put The Canadian Back In Bacon"*) **prepare a slideshow for potential franchisees in Ohio**. The consultant and Slappy collaborate using Google Presentations, which lets them remotely access the deck and add text, images, and other elements. The consultant shares a link to the slideshow with her consulting partner, so he can periodically review it on a Web browser and check for problems. Later, Slappy meets his potential franchise operators at a hotel in Cleveland, and uses Presentations to run through the slides.

- **An elementary school faculty uses Google Documents to collaborate on lesson plans.** Each teacher accesses the same document from their homes or classrooms. Updates are instantly reflected, even when two teachers are simultaneously accessing the same document. Their principal (known as "Skinner" behind his back) is impressed by how quickly the faculty completes the plans, and how well the curriculums are integrated.

- At the same school, the 5th-grade teachers **ask their students to submit homework using Documents**. The teachers add corrections and notes, which the students can access at any time via a Web browser. It's much more efficient than emailing attachments around, and the students don't need to bug their parents to buy expensive word-processing programs.

Many people try Google Docs because it's free (Google Drive is, too, if you store less than five gigabytes of data). Microsoft Office can cost hundreds of dollars, and the programs in Apple's iWork suite cost nearly $60. While Google Docs is not as sophisticated, it handles the basics very well. Docs also offers a slew of powerful online features that are unmatched by Office or iWork, including:

- The ability to review the history of a specific document, and revert to an earlier version.

- Simple Web forms and online surveys which can be produced

without programming skills or website hosting arrangements.

- Collaboration features that let users work on the same document in real time.

- Offline file storage that can be synced to multiple computers.

- Automatic notification of the release date of Brad Pitt's next movie.

I'm just kidding about the last item. But Google Drive and Docs really can do those other things, and without the help of your company's IT department or the pimply teenager from down the street. These features are built right into the software, and are ready to use as soon as you've signed up.

Even though the myriad features of Google Drive may seem overwhelming, this guide makes it easy to get started. *Google Drive & Docs In 30 Minutes* is written in plain English, with lots of step-by-step instructions, screenshots and tips. More resources are available on the companion website to this book, DriveDocsIn30Minutes.com. You'll get up to speed in no time.

We've only got a half-hour, so let's get started with Google Drive and Docs!

If you want to continue reading, visit the official book website located at DriveDocsIn30Minutes.com.

Bonus: Introduction To Excel Basics In 30 Minutes

(The following chapter is from Excel Basics In 30 Minutes. *If you're interested in buying a copy, visit the official book website at ExcelIn30Minutes.com.)*

Some years ago, a colleague came over to my cubicle and asked for some help. John wanted to create a long list of names, categorize them, and assign a score on a scale of one to 10 for each one. Then, he wanted to do things with the list, such as identifying the top scores and creating category averages.

John knew I was familiar with all kinds of desktop and online software. He asked, "Which one would you recommend for this type of task?"

"That's easy," I answered. "Enter the data into Microsoft Excel or Google Spreadsheets. You can then alphabetize the list, sort by the highest and lowest scores, and draw out category averages. You can even create neat-looking charts based on the results." I used Excel to whip up a basic list, and emailed him the file.

John thanked me profusely, but admitted, "I have only the vaguest idea about and almost no experience with spreadsheets."

John's situation is not unusual. Millions of people know that Excel can be used for tracking financial data and number crunching. They may have even opened Excel and entered some numbers into a corporate expense worksheet.

Nevertheless, Excel suffers from an image problem. Most people assume that spreadsheet programs such as Excel are intended for accountants, analysts, financiers, scientists, mathematicians, and other geeky types. Creating a spreadsheet, sorting data, using functions, and making charts seems daunting, and best left to the nerds.

I'm here to tell you that spreadsheets are *not* just for nerds. Practically anyone can use Excel for work, school, personal projects and other uses. I've written this guide to help you quickly get up to speed on basic concepts, using plain English, step-by-step instructions, and lots of screenshots. Thirty minutes from now, you'll know how to:

- Create a spreadsheet and enter numbers and text into cells.

- Perform addition, multiplication, and other simple mathematical functions.

- Derive values based on percentages.

- Perform time-saving tasks, such as sorting large lists and automatically applying the same formula across a range of values.

- Make great-looking charts.

You can imagine how these techniques can help in real-world situations, from tracking household expenses to making sales projections. You can even use them to organize events, and track the office football pool.

We only have 30 minutes, so let's get started!

(To learn more about Excel Basics In 30 Minutes *and watch free online videos, visit ExcelIn30Minutes.com.)*